salmonpoetry

Diverse Voices from Ireland and the World

Ecstatic

Kevin Higgins

Published in 2022 by
Salmon Poetry
Cliffs of Moher, County Clare, Ireland
Website: www.salmonpoetry.com
Email: info@salmonpoetry.com

ISBN 978-1-915022-14-1

Cover image: *"Kevin Higgins portrait" by Christopher Banahan.*
Technique: fresco fragment. Size: 21 x 22 inches. Christopherbanahan.wordpress.com

Cover Design & Typesetting: *Siobhán Hutson*

Printed in Ireland by Sprint Print

*Salmon Poetry gratefully acknowledges the support of
The Arts Council / An Chomhairle Ealaíon*

for Julian & Stella Assange

Contents

Never

after Alfonso Gatto

The dread of being together
    forcing us back to sleep.
The sewer pipes are
    our murderer clearing his throat.
And light not needed by the day,
    throwing itself uselessly against
the sea-salted window pane,
    leaves evidence of itself
on the prehistoric carpet.
    Animal sounds. Then words
we don't yet know the meaning of.
    Each still behind their mask
not yet quite alive. The hours refusing to pass
    for fear this might amount to more
than a thought two ex-people once had
    in private. And never dared
sing out in chorus.

Nothing

after Edward Thomas

The soot of evening tumbles
to Earth turning the street to nothing.
A mad old woman – or what sounds
like a mad old woman – with a bony voice
trapped down the chimney accuses
the world of once again letting the children
feed a nest load of magpie chicks
to the black cat. The cat, if it exists,
doesn't care, its mouth full of meat
and blue blue feathers. Nothing
is what it was half an hour ago.
The bicycle chained to the lamppost
has temporarily ceased to exist.
The restaurants are secretly
full of couples who tonight will dream
they're driving a small red car
to their lover's funeral,
or what they think is their lover's funeral.

Winter Coupling

He was a knock knock knocking cough
to which most of a man
was still theoretically attached.
She was as anxious as a cat
with arthritis in its elbows, thrown
among the pit-bull pups next door.
That solstice, it had been so long
since they'd tried intercourse
they had to use a Ouija board,
and employ a strange lady from Moravia,
dressed all in harlequin green,
to guide their papery, grey hands
zero to nine across it,
and commune
with the spirit of their springtime.

People I Almost Slept With

The memory of our lovemaking is the Olympic medal
the leading middle-distance runner
of my Irish childhood doesn't have
in his cabinet to remind him
– winter nights –
of his moment of triumph
because he kept finishing fourth.

Our unzipping each
other's trousers with our teeth
was the opportunity
we were both forever
failing to leap on.

We came close
as the Dutch national soccer team of the seventies
did to winning successive world cups.

The nanosecond we first
put eyes on each other, the world
settled back on its hideous orange sofa
and waited for the inevitable to,
in the end,
not actually happen. In the finish

we were Robert Rensenbrink's flick
coming magically
back off the post,
last minute of injury time,
and him learning
the true meaning of never
getting his hands
on that most lusted after
piece of eighteen carat gold.

Or, to abuse a different euphemism,
our time in bed together was like
the French restaurant
we fully intended to visit,
but which seemed to deliberately close
whenever we were both in town.

We'll forever wonder what it would've been like:
the table under our eager elbows;
the chairs embracing our twitching behinds;
the leather feel of the menus
as our fingers moved nervously
across the list between
L'Escargot and Coq Au Vin;

we'll never know exactly what either
would have tasted like.

Diary of an Absurdist

This is not the usual route I'd take
to the place I never go.

I spend the holidays I don't have
listening to the albums
John Lennon would've made,
if he hadn't been shot.

My head's full of ways
back down mountains
I never intend to climb.

Anytime you want to talk
call me on the telephone
I just had disconnected.

I was once made violently ill
by a cheese-steak
I plan to one day eat.

I'm a big fan of the books
Paulo Coehlo didn't live to write.

Come see me Christmas morning
for some eggnog and sauerkraut.
I'll definitely be out.

Not Yet

after Hans Magnus Enzensberger

I'm sat here heroically
thinking about perhaps having
another buttered fruit scone.
The family animal dozes
on the giant leather sofa
I bought for it. It is not yet
time to commit suicide again.

The galvanised roof
hasn't yet blown off
the shed I inherited
from Mother. The light bulb over
the front door would work,
if I chose to switch it on.
The car alarm
has been silenced for now.

That the evening might finish up
in my favourite restaurant
remains a theoretical possibility.
The scented candle hasn't yet
set the curtains on fire.
And Germany has yet
to be re-partitioned.

I am still in a position
to deny everything.

A hearse comes gleaming
through the evening traffic
with no body in it.

What am I waiting for?

Metaphor

You'd feel the shadow of it,
like where you had a wound before.
The enemy would target the injury,
the weak spot, that's where
the flare up will occur.
The shadow would say:
I am what you must carry with you.

I can see the pinker tissue around it
and the darker, more jagged tissue,
like a bad scar on your hand that remains visible.
It's heavy, and you are lifting it.
Rather than being springy like lungs are supposed to be,
it's like an old mattress with no support in it.

It became something that couldn't be ignored,
took over where the old drama left off.
The solicitor was replaced by the doctor.
I found it hard to care about anything.

Cold weather makes things contract.
Close weather too. Like in a room where
there's no through air.
My mother when she was dying would say:
"Open the window. Open the window!"
Like a barometer, I know if it is a heavy day.
Like people do with sinuses.

If there's a curveball and Friday is a heavy day,
I will get a cough way down.
So far down, it causes me to throw up.
Susan hears me coughing in the bathroom
trying to clear something from way down.

I can feel it there now.
Like something that is working now
but you can feel where the tear was.
When you've been in the war.
And something is not right.

Conversation

Your shoulders fall softly
as if you're gazing down a hole
to see if you can see water
or at least the bottom of the hole
in what might be
yourself. But you can't
make it out exactly.
Perhaps you need new glasses.

Times like this you are soft
as the snail you met yesterday
while it was slithering
down your garden wall
minding its own business
and you stopped
to touch, very gently.
And it stopped
its slithering as if to say:
"Who the fuck is yer man?!"

Before going about its business
as you clicked open
the lock on the garden gate
to go about yours.

Two stones.
One male, grey, and absolute
telling the world: "Here I am.
I can take any boot put down on me."

The other so white
smooth faced
it looks almost soft.
Its hidden side ridged with complications.

If you trod on it barefoot on the beach
it could break and make you bleed.
And you'd recoil like a snail
going back into its shell.

That's the risk,
and you take it.

Black Winter Tree

The black winter tree is my lungs
is my lungs
is nothing like my lungs
for it will remain
long after my lungs
have been put away
like the carcass of Thursday's roast chicken.

I bring my lungs
to the black winter tree
and it gives us
our latest results.

What the black winter tree breathes out
I try to breathe in.
But my lungs only take me
halfway there.

The black winter tree remembers
my mother
and will remember me.

The black winter tree watched
my grandparents leave
after the final table-banging argument.

Each time Venus
punched me in the stomach
to emphasise her refusal
the black winter tree muttered:
"Well, that went well, didn't it."

Whenever some fresh bit of paradise
is lost, the black winter tree
is there to remind me
I'm still alive.

Sympathy for The Leaves

Praise the thick roots of the tree:
who you are,
who you were,
who you will be.
That which you never see
and often forget,
rough days, keeps you standing here.
For not everything is planted
in the stone flecked earth
you stand in.

Pity the leaves,
those who know not
what throws them about
and out of the garden.
Their whispers
are not opinions
but what way the wind
is sending them just now.

Execution

Oh tree, I thought, metaphor
for my life.
For you were my lungs
in black x-ray
against white winter sky.
You were everlasting
as the granite boulder
still stubbornly making its point
underneath our house.
But also now as temporary as hope
or an Emperor of China.

For Wednesday morning came the chainsaws,
ordered in like airstrikes
by the neighbour
on whose patch you grew
and a committee of fat men
and worthy ladies
who go by the name
Galway City Council.

So reduced when they left,
metaphor only for the times my finger
told the world what it thinks of it,
or my most embarrassing part
rose to greet the thought
of the girl at number fifteen
who by now must be
applying for her bus pass.

You, stump, are metaphor perfected –
for new reduced–to–clear me –
cleansed of high ideas
by the saws' grinning teeth.

What's Following Me

These days, I'm followed everywhere
by my own skeleton.

I see it looking out at me
from the windows of buses
on their way to places I once lived,
or clattering about
the break-time playgrounds
of schools I used to
occasionally attend.

In the butcher's shop
I spot it, a few
behind me in the queue.
It tails me, at an increasingly
indiscreet distance,
all the way home.

In the doctor's waiting room
it sits right across from me
and clacks its jaws
with the confidence of one
who already knows
the diagnosis.

After making what felt like
love, I glance across at the chair
on which we left most of our clothes
and it's sitting there,
with exactly the right number
of missing teeth.

Some nights it grabs my arm;
hisses that it'll soon help me free myself
from all this disgusting flesh.

For Eros, An Elegy

Her hands are a safety harness
that will not hold you.
The hair on her head is a field
let return to the wild despite complaints
and solicitor's letters from neighbours.
Her droopy right eyelid is the shutter
on a sex-shop, eager
to close for the evening.

Her chest is the hills of Clare
inviting you across the bay;
though you can't swim
and the last boat has left
for the season. Her neck, lips, and ears
are the menu of starters
in a restaurant so fabulous
the security guards are paid a bonus
to eject the likes of you.

Her spine is a repossessed grand piano
you still play to yourself
in your sleep. Her pubic hair
is a lawn you'll never get to
walk across or break into a sweat
mowing. Her bum-hole is a sweet-
factory you'll never be allowed visit.
And the cheeks either side of it
smoother than the nectarines
you remember from July.

Her thighs are piping hot
turkey on the table for Christmas,
though with a far better
personality than your average turkey.
And between them all the oranges
stomach acid no longer allows you to eat.

Blindfold

after Robert Desnos

I have pictured her so long,
around my idea of her has grown
an actual woman. Her hair black
as the shirt ripped off the back
of Mussolini's last bodyguard;
her eyes grey as the inside
of a padlocked mausoleum;
her nose perfect as the Golden Gate Bridge,
though not quite as big;
her hands bobbing about in air
like the first Magnolia flowers of the year;
the ankle she twisted on a broken
paving stone while trying to escape
a nightmare for which
I wrote the script.

So long I have worn this blindfold
that blocks out everything
but my imaginings of her,
I know I'll one day sleep
with the prostheses she'll have to get
when old and diabetic
because of all the sweets
I fed her in my dreams.

Should

after Czeslaw Milosz

A man should not spend too long crouching in the corner
of his own cupboard. Even the people he lives with
will forget he's there. Every cupboard, in time,
gets taken away. Some of them to not nice places,
such as Ardrahan or Dudley North.

A man shouldn't spend too long sharpening the same axe
before either using it to solve the situation, or putting it
aside to roll about naked in a field full of thistles.
Thistles that spring up like arguments with buried
relatives and visitors who outstayed their welcome.

When psychiatrists, or counsels for the prosecution,
ask him to paint a picture of what happened,
a man should leave ninety percent of the canvas blank,
for them to fill in themselves later.
It's what they'll do anyway.

A man should put more in society's envelope
than news of his latest infection.
He should not install curry stains
on other people's settees,
or pretend he knows how to fix washing machines.

A man should not wait until during the storm
to climb up and count his roof tiles;
should avoid scrambling to great heights
to then prove to himself
what the pavement can do
just by being itself.

Ecstatic

"Have you ever seen me ecstatic? Well this is it."
Estelle, Joey's agent on *Friends*

I'm ecstatic, honeybunch,
at the idea of you still out there
doing impressions of yourself
or whoever the moment demands you be.

When the latest release landed
from your Department of Propaganda
I was so ecstatic at the sound of you
pretending to be serious, I spat

my tea out from laughing
at that and the now requisite photo
of what you allegedly
had for breakfast;

the plate full of things
to which you told me
you're allergic.

Come see me,
when a rare blank day
opens up on your calendar;

pick, please, cleanly as you can
my eyes out with this giant tweezers
and let local crows feast

on them, so I no longer
have to look at you,
or you, or you, or you...

Heaven

after Cathy Song

I think when we die I go back to Coventry,
a version where it's permanently 1973.
Where my cousin, Mary, is permanently five
and not yet our accountant.
We play cowboys and Indians
with small, plastic figurines who ride
tiny plastic horses. And the world is exactly
as it should be.

Where I'm permanently the miniature man
in the passenger seat of my Dad's van
as we roar up the A45
to our weekly Thursday evening shop
at the One Stop on the verge of Birmingham.

Where I'm permanently playing
for the first time *Sean South of Garryowen,*
slightly out of sync with the others,
on my new button accordion
on the big stage at the Kerryman's Club.

Where I'm permanently tumbling backwards
through the kitchen door's glass
for the Sunday evening entertainment
of the entire family
and acquiring the one scar
that's on the outside.

Where the old lady at the end of our street
is permanently putting
Vote Conservative in her front window
and I have no need to hate her.
The car factories down the road –
Rolls Royce, Chrysler, Jaguar –

are, in any case, permanently ruining
every other day for her
by walking "all out!", on a show of hands.
The Secretary of State for Education
is permanently Margaret Hilda Thatcher, and despite
her technically being in charge of boys my size,
I've never heard of her.

Where I'm permanently learning my first few focal
in preparation for our return
to the place Mom and Dad call home.
I'm permanently correcting my tutor
for putting County Clare
in the wrong province of Connacht,
and at the age of barely six
am disgustingly pleased with myself.

Where everyone in our family
is still miraculously
talking to everyone else.
And the world is permanently
as it should be.

On Receiving A Text From A Once Friend

after Lord Byron

So, we'll sit no more circle jerking
our tiny minds uselessly out
with no conclusion, political or otherwise,
though the afternoon is far from cooked and this hand
prepared to power past its chronic arthritis.

The average head outlives many crash helmets.
We'd now happily feed each other to compost heaps.
For disdain must be allowed gnaw
itself down to shreds, like dissatisfied beetles.

Though the future is made of hair loss
and things getting gradually smaller,
we sit, two shrivelled factions trying
to imagine our own continued existence.
Though all the light-bulbs have long blown,
we can still hear each other muttering
in our walled apart dark.

A Great Uncle

after R.S. Thomas

Matt to familiars, Maloney to his enemies;
the book of whom was fat and ancient
and always being written. One word
accidentally out of place and you'd
get life without parole
on the version of Devil's Island
he had purpose built in his head.

He'd enter a room like
the premature onset of twilight.
Whiskey chasers in the brown saloon
bars of Headford and Shrule
quickened him, fixed
his anger's shotgun on its preferred targets.
Though he never killed anyone
that way. That incidental
whose head went against a kerbstone
came in for an argument, and got served one.

The Tuam Herald and *Western People*
taken into back rooms and read
away from the eyes of children.
Manslaughter. Sentence suspended.
The accused's exemplary life
and two elderly parents
who must be cared for.

They die. He sells
first cattle, then land.
Tired of driving wonky green vans
off the same old roads
and having to be rescued.
England. The lodging houses
of West London. New Year's Eve
arguments picked with visitors
about the naming of nephew and nieces.

That nursing home, and antiseptic
death in a different century.

Next Door

after Zbigniew Herbert

The devil next door lives mostly
in the cubbyhole under the staircase
with a bag of Christmas decorations
which are awaiting execution,
two lampshades of questionable parentage,
and half a tin of past-it varnish.

The devil next door has tragic blue eyes
it stole from my grandmother
during one of her episodes.

The devil next door only comes out
when the woman of the house
has the place to herself,
gives her the words
she hurls at passing schoolchildren,
all of whom are me.

His handshake is Musk thistle
and his voice depressed mice;
as he waltzes her
red jacket everyone laughed at
round and round the living room.

The devil next door has the mouth
of the man her uncle accidentally killed
and breath cold as Nineteen Forty Seven.

She tosses him scraps of raw liver
when there's nobody about.
In return he keeps her supplied
with dead birds to chuck over the fence
at her nieces and nephew,
so we never forget who we are.

The Goddess of Gossip

after Bertolt Brecht

She flew in and perched next to me
in the coffee shop today,
flashed me some papers she said
gave her the legal right
to take possession of my head.

She breathed all over me
and I inhaled all the cigarettes she's lit up
and will continue to devour
long after I'm dead;
introduced me to her sidekick
who materialised beside her –
a bald dwarf who talked
but said nothing
and wouldn't stop smiling.

In her disintegrating voice
she croaked
how she was on my side,
and my wife's side too,
then asked me
the colour of my underpants.
I joked I wasn't wearing any.
Her sidekick muttered
neither was he
scribbled something
in his tiny pink notebook.

And the chimney of her mouth
continued to blow
how she's a great champion of me,
my wife, and all belonging to me;
that's why she keeps a close,
if slightly wonky, eye on my enemies

and my wife's enemies
and my late mother's enemies
who one of my neighbours
had told her all about.

As a professional lady might reveal
her left tit to an auctioneer
in town for the Galway Races
in the hope he'll pay for a look
at the other one, she threw
morsels of truth
on the table between us.
And when I ate none of them,
Sidekick scratched another note
in his little pink book
and chuckled to himself.

Barely audible now,
her good eye superglued to the door
as if it was expecting someone important,
she leaned in
and reassured me
her presence in my life
and in my wife's life
and in the lives of all belonging to me
would be shortlived
and entirely benign.

For The One Who Has Lived
Too Little and Too Long

after George Hitchcock

I wait for the ruin inherent in every building
to emerge triumphant;
I wait for the eight foot tall woman to stop dancing
around my mind with her three foot tall man;
I wait for the blood test that might be the beginning of a solution.

I wait for the recently widowed magpie
to alight brutally on the garden fence;
I wait for the handcuffs and laxatives;
I wait for the doctor to try not to frown
and choose her words very carefully.

I wait for this particular mouse-trap
to embrace its prey in its jaws;
I wait for the Sanity Protection Office
to respond to my letter about the world's failure
to stop reminding me you're still in it;
I wait for the car alarms to not let you sleep
and the morphine to not quite work;
I wait for the skeleton to be set free from its flesh.

I wait for the kidneys and heart
to be sold to a buyer in, we think, Tajikistan;
I wait for the bed sheets and mattress
to be taken out and burnt;
I wait for the specially extended
extra long coffin, I've been
ecstatically hammering together for you.

In the Alleyways

after Charlotte Mew

Reader, when I glimpse the stray
        bits of latex that glitter in alleyways
under the bare honesty
        of out of season trees,
or watch the necessary liquids
        slime down the fish factory gully;
how could I believe
        there are truer things on Earth than these?
When I bring you back here,
        years from now, you'll admit
there's likely nothing more beautiful
        than the briefly living things
who come at nightfall
        with the arguing starlings
and the scent of cod and chips
        up alleyways they still frequent
though it's winter.

Two Rooms

after Charlotte Mew

The world is rooms that open into other
rooms. One minute
the relative safety of Venetian blinds
and the Christmas tree falling down.
The next, that bed-sit kitchenette
where you can take up
drinking gin, decide
to set up your own
abattoir, or
think about joining
a charisma for beginners class;

not care
about the black lino
in the corner of your new
world where the previous tenant
used to light fires to express his
disappointment at how
things had turned out:

his wit a tin opener
that hadn't worked in years, the day
the Future came to say:
Nothing personal.
We just think you're
unnecessary.

Advice From An Irish Poet To The People of Delaware

"Delaware is the least visited state in the U.S."

TheCultureTrip.com

Do something desperate.
Then, years from now, charge people to come remember it.
Employ a local enthusiast as the 'Wilmington Throttler'.
Allow him prowl your less desirable neighbourhoods
doing what his nickname implies.
Then name a popular TV series and walking tour after him.
Or let Joe Biden corral his opponents
into Delaware Sportsplex, wire
their bits up to the mains and let
starving police dogs at them.
Within fifty years you'll be
the Santiago of the North.

There are other models you might follow:
Cambodia, for example,
would today have little to attract
its ever increasing carnival
of tattooed backpackers,
if Brother Number One hadn't
the foresight to number
and photograph
all 1,386,734 enemies of the people
before they were processed.

And where would the economy of West Mayo be,
if the god-sent blight hadn't brought
lines of Famine hungry Japanese tourists
to trek across the calcium deficient
bones of our ancestors.

As the old Irish saying says:
whatever you do, admit everything.
For no one hates Holocaust denial more
than the old woman who runs a bed and breakfast
five miles from Auschwitz.

Sensualist Resolutions

after Tim Emlyn Jones

Drink whiskey not because you think
it'll fix your personality
but because the first sip always tastes
like the best glass of smoke available
this side of Hell, and makes your throat dream
of tomorrow morning's pint
glass of water helping down
the greasiest bacon sandwich
in the history of grease.

Treat yourself to the occasional cigar
not because anyone's granny said
there's nothing like it
to clear out your lungs
but because, in a certain light –
namely the dark – it makes you look like
Che Guevara, if he'd lived
to lose ninety per cent of his hair.

Embrace the bitterness
of black tea without a single grain of sugar,
drink disgustingly strong coffee,
let it tarnish all your teeth.
And never sniff a bed sheet
or pair of knickers
for anything other than the sheer
aesthetic thrill of it.

Helmet

His wife was like Prince Charles,
only with far bigger ears.
The day of their wedding,
at her mother's insistence,
he took out a second mortgage to fix them,
though they were his favourite part of her;
then a third to pay for the lawyer
when the operation went horribly wrong;
a fourth to buy the designer crash helmet
she wore everywhere
while awaiting the court case,
even when making love,

or sucking untipped high tar cigarettes,
or boarding planes to Eritrea
where they holidayed regularly.
She never removed that helmet
until the day of his cremation,
when she threw it,
like a bowling ball,
into the incinerator with him;
revealed
her ears miraculously healed.

Love Song of Hercule Poirot

after David Gascoyne

There is a catastrophe of dandelion clocks
in the greenhouse where our orchids live
and the murder was meant to take place.
The village librarian will have to be telephoned
and told we'll throttle her some other time.
From under my purple dressing gown, the smell
of middle aged picnic ham and Timotei shampoo.
Your arms are miniature dancing chainsaws,
but I waltz around the room with you anyway,
though you always confiscate a few chunks
of meat from my back. You are forever
sawing off shotguns while wearing
only sunglasses, with one lens missing;
or threatening to use your pet
flamethrower on the postman;

and when you're not
you're writing letters to Von Ribbentrop
offering him your assistance.
Until interrupted by the click of the garden gate,
like a safety catch being taken off,
as the librarian arrives for her rescheduled date
with the bit of wire you spent the morning polishing.

The Ten Great Wisdoms

Wit is a cocktail
in which the final ingredient
is a pair of scissors in the eye.
Patience is a wasp
wrestling a Bristol United supporter
for the last glass of cider in all Gloucestershire.
Reliability is a car with arthritis
and no steering wheel
on Corkscrew Hill.
Opinion is a dildo
made of several different flavours of ice-cream.
Politics is the choice between a cod-piece
that never fulfils its promise,
and a fridge full of amputated hands
that always keeps its.
Respite is HP Sauce,
or what you hope is HP Sauce,
and old episodes of Dr Who
in the Home for The Funny Peculiar.
Clarification is a debate between a watermelon
and an AK47 on a tablecloth so white
the Ku Klux Klan tried to steal it.
Discretion is a body which, impressively,
has not yet been found.
Your face, wondering where all this is going,
is the main street of a town
the day it's everybody's funeral
including yours.

Truth is a paper-cut
no one but you knows is there.

Note left behind in abandoned psychiatric hospital

after anon: nineteenth century

Oh what my thoughts did here with my mechanised cheese-grater.
For the neck of my lust had been snapped like a digestive biscuit.
The cold lentil curry went screaming to the floor
and, as the sobbing contents of those dishes slimed
my path, the shaved cat mooed to itself like an elk.
Tomorrow's immaculate corduroy pants have been torn off me,
are vanished as a heroine who only exists in songs
once shouted through teeth now full of thistles and clay.

And yet, why should I leap obediently into this coffin?
Or find for you the electrified Brillo pad they pretended to wash me with?
Or entertain you by chasing the fat bacon around your plate?
Or chew for you this big white pill you insist is a mint?
Never, Mephistopheles, not while your lips against mine
are a plucked chicken being once again burned alive because it's Thursday.

My Preoccupation

after Henri Michaux

Since it happened,
everyone I talk to
longer than five minutes
I wonder which side they'd take
if cornered by fate,
history, a smiling chequebook
or policeman, as we all eventually will be?

Men and women I overhear in the coffee shop
I immediately find guilty,
though they will have the right
to go to the Court of Appeal,
if I haven't abolished it
by the time their case comes up.

Look at that one over there!
I am taking a sip from my tea mug
and scratching onto the back of an envelope
I happen to have on me
a warrant for his arrest.

This one beside me, I acquit,
despite certain initial reservations.

But listen to her over there.
Already she is being led
down to the cells
and treated according to the letter
of what will then be the Law.

Get over it, they tell me.
But I'm still pissed about the Menai Massacre
of Sixty One A.D., never mind
what was done to me in nineteen ninety four.

Vengeance is a cup of hot and sour soup
best gulped down before
the potential war criminal has time
to iron his or her new uniform
and disarm you with their banter.

Let bygones be written
in permanent marker on their gravestones.

When a Serial Killer Dies

Beelzebub's eyes
leak tar tears at this latest one's
paucity of ambition, the way he settled
for the petty pennies of taking
a ragged chainsaw to the moist necks
of particular children in a disused
wine cellar when, if only he'd
had the farsightedness to leave
the local playgrounds to themselves

he could've been
Secretary of State for Defence;
bought for himself, with money
that'd otherwise have been wasted
on old people, the ability to set fire
to the Suez Canal or Antarctica;
had named after him a bomb
smart enough to go to Oxford,
instead of the imminent
twenty five past midnight
film for television;

perhaps been the diplomat
who dismembered like earthworms
Africa and Arabia into manageable,
symmetrical segments and had
a small country and scholarship
to his old college
set up in his honour;

matured into the General who bravely
pacified Indochina and Mesopotamia,
like a schoolboy methodically
tearing the legs off a spider
in the quiet of his bedroom -

the twelfth so far today –
and had so many medals
pinned on his chest, in the end
he almost fell over;

or been the peace envoy
who oversaw the evacuation
of the last German speakers from Danzig,
watched them stream
down country roads like ants,

after that made a living
telling university students
how he did it.

Dishonest Doris

You apportion blame for your life
like a nun spreading strawberry jam in wartime,
taking care never to get any on yourself.
Deep in your cranium a gramophone record spins
the case for your own acquittal:

that it's not your fault
your psychiatrist no longer returns your calls,
or that his predecessor resigned
and leapt cackling into
the deadliest bit of the river.

In the matter of all
the potential ex-husbands
who joined silent monastic orders
under false names, or paid vast sums
to have themselves neutered
by some back-street carving knife,
in each and every instance, the verdict:
them, not you.

As for the kittens you keep adopting,
every one of which absconds
first time you let it out for a run,
unfriends you on Facebook and makes
straight for the motorway
where it pleads with heavy goods vehicles
to squish it;

your supreme court of one
puts on its big, dusty wig
and pronounces
everyone guilty but you,
ungrateful kittens included.

Towards A Dennis O'Driscoll Re-write of A Cesare Pavese Poem

Stupid takes after you, its smirk
the one you wear while confidently doing
whatever it is you do worst.

You wouldn't recognise stupid
if it superglued your eyes open,
threw a bucket of water on you, and sang
"I am what I am" in your ear
with a megaphone.

Stupid can give you a back rub
from the other end of a crowded room.

When stupid comes it will be wearing a coat
made of ideas it stole from you.

Stupid points a water pistol at you
and demands the handover
of your head in its entirety.

Stupid opens your skull with a mechanised
tin opener and goes for a walk inside.

Then stupid takes the steering wheel
and starts driving your thoughts
down motorways at twice
whatever the speed limit is.

Stupid will take your brain
from its box and marshal it
into a circus act that'll make
people leap laughing onto train tracks.

Stupid will take your history and give it
to TV comedy panel shows to rewrite.

Stupid lashes out at all your best ideas
until they lie, a defenceless mush,
on the autopsy table.

Stupid cries on shoulders
that are not its to cry on.

You are up to your raised eyebrows
in stupid.

The Art of Collaboration

Whatever job he's given,
the collaborator is a perfect fit.
A man of no fixed particulars.
His views are plastic
and always on the verge
of being melted down
and made otherwise.
His life is a full orchestra
of raised eyebrows
and suppressed twitches.
The collaborator laughs at your jokes
and makes it look like he means it.

Whatever it is,
the collaborator makes it his business.
He writes everything down,
especially your name.
The collaborator is awake tonight
and looking up the number
of the relevant government agency
so he can phone them tomorrow to tell them
what he's heard you've been doing.
The collaborator doesn't mind being put on hold.

The collaborator knows
the name of the woman, man, emu
you were with in that hotel room
you shouldn't have been in.

The collaborator points the nice policeman
in the direction of those
the newspapers say are bad men (and women).
For the collaborator doesn't discriminate,
except in favour of himself.

Always and Everywhere

after Wislawa Szymborska

God may have been abolished
but politics is everywhere and always.
Your arrival on and departure from
Earth are political.
Even if you don't die of it,
though many do,
politics is present at your last breath
as it was for your first.

For some people,
wearing their hair a certain length
so others will presume
they were against certain wars
is the most political thing they've ever done.
For them, not getting that haircut
was a personal revolution which continued
long after they got private health insurance
and had tomorrow's Washington Post op-ed
preinstalled in their brains.

In other countries,
what colour laces you use
to do up your boots with
is politics of the most serious variety;
as is the fact across most of the planet
it's legal to kill a wasp
with the local equivalent of The Irish Times
but not yet to take a lump hammer
to an auctioneer.

And that those on distant
and, presumably, better worlds,
who must be able to see enough of us
to pity us,
can't be bothered to come rescue us
from ourselves
until there's something in it for them
is politics at its intergalactic worst.

Equality

Admit
you're against it,
that what you mean
when you say it is yourself
being let in the door –
toodlepip –
of the best room
to sink your glutes
into one of its more
distinguished armchairs
and be heard
finally via a microphone
that can never be turned off.
That equality is paying someone else
7.50 an hour, instead
of being paid it yourself,
is not got
by people devoid of deodorant
ransacking the sideboard ornaments
and taking it for themselves
but given
in small, appropriate doses
by committees of people like you
in possession of microphones
that can never be turned off.

Ultimate Bathroom Experience

The bathrooms of Late Capitalism differ
from the bathrooms of feudalism
and the bathrooms of the industrial revolution
in that they exist.
No more throwing it
out into the street
in the hope of hitting the neighbour
you argued with yesterday.

As you depart
the bathrooms of Late Capitalism
the attendant tries to sell you
bottles of your own widdle, jars
of what you worked so hard
to make, labelled *Organic*.
When they succeed
you feel like you came away
with a great bargain.

The perfect skin cream
for the Father's Day market
to help them stop withering
in the face of Late Capitalism;
a dressing to drizzle
on your favourite salad
to stop it wilting
in the light of
Late Capitalism; the perfect
pep me up

days you've visited the doctor
and been told: Madam,
it's Late Capitalism.
But, tragically,
not terminal.
On your way out
kindly swipe your card
on the relevant part
of the receptionist
and continue to the exit.

What I'm Like

Lively as an elderly blue-arsed fly
that's just been clattered by
the weekend edition of the New York Times.
About as much use in a debate about anything
as a weighing scale floating through outer space.
Reassuring as a naked funeral director
stepping into the same hot tub as you
in search of new customers.
My future smells delicious
as the used odour-eaters
I was going to send you for Christmas
until I saw the price of the postage.
My dream, that little children of every
complexion and gender
will one day gather together
to play Frisbee with stray toilet seat lids
they plucked from the rubble.

Their Return

The people who lived here before,
we slowly abolish them
by buying beaming new fridges,
washer dryers, cookers
with fan ovens that actually work
and two year warranties, more sofas
for the cat to do Tai Chi on.

Yet the rooms are loaded
with the thought of them.
We tear up the garden they grew here
and plant shrubs that speak of us.

Yet the air is full
of the things they believed,
and the things they'll say about us
when they come back.

In Memoriam: the worst public toilet in Galway

Hidden like a pimple on the City's most intimate bit.
We went down your steps to tiles
that were never white and had seen things
no lavatory attendant should have to look at.

You hung above the river
as it went viciously about its business.
Whatever the temperature
you were ten degrees less.
No one visited you except out of desperation
or via the sort of mistake American tourists make.

You belonged to gents in questionable coats
with even more questionable things
hanging hopefully beneath them
like ukuleles.

Though you've been boarded up
since what's now the last century; it's said
each Halloween and Macnas parade,
in your far dark, their coats come alive
to again disgrace your tiles.

For Michael O'Leary

after Primo Levi

You are everywhere and, when it matters, nowhere
oh Lord of this cancelled flight.
All across a continent the bodies pile up
at Ryanair help desks while you are home
talking to your horses who are grateful
they, at least, will never have to travel
Ryanair. I don't want you taken to the termination chamber
some here are building for you, or pulled apart before
a jeering crowd by the four of your own racehorses
with the most unresolved anger management issues.
May you live to be a thousand years old
and spend your remaining nine hundred and forty two
years sweating in a queue to speak to a red faced girl
at a Ryanair help desk. Let your every night be Sunday
and it always be December. May you be late
to the death bed and cremation
of your favourite uncle and his remains
be delivered to you
while you're still here in this queue,
in a clear plastic bag with a hole in it,
for which you will, naturally, be charged.
And when you open your mouth
and a complainy word shoots out
may the Chilean secret police instantly appear
and tell you with their eyes,
and their drooling Alsatians' eyes,
to cut that out or your slug tongue
will no longer be yours to wiggle.
And when your time here is done
may you be peeled, tied,
and spread-eagled across your own help desk
and two fat blokes from Chipping Ongar
be paid to sprinkle pollen
all over you, and then release
the bees.

Priti Patel's Denial

"I just wanted to hear [them] deny it."
Lyndon Baines Johnson

It is not true that at our meeting today
I forced the Foreign Secretary and
Chancellor of the Duchy of Lancaster to bathe
in piping hot custard and gently
scrubbed their backs, bellies, balls
with my bristling, steel wire-brush
until they were strip-loin raw
and roaring to God
for me to stop.

The whole thing was their idea in the first place.

Nor do I make
the Secretary of State for Work and Pensions
wear a gimp suit to all day
meetings, during which I only unzip the mouth
to feed it occasional morsels
of uranium washed chicken kebab
with my long hot fork.

She turns up dressed like that entirely of her own volition.

And the rumours I ram
an electric hair straightener
with a loose connection
up parts of the Secretary of State for Wales
not designed to take
an electric hair straightener
with a loose connection
have been vastly exaggerated.

Said implement was in excellent working order.
I even took care to wipe the remnants
of the last guy off it.

Nor is there, for the most part,
any reality to online accusations
that at our most recent
meeting I covered the Attorney General
toe to forehead in cats' blood
and locked him in a closet
to be fought over by my pet
Staffordshire bull terrier, Enoch
and a one eyed East African wild dog
called Field Marshall Idi Amin
I keep around the place
just in case.

The closet you speak of remained unlocked
during the entire process
which my Right Honourable friend appeared to
thoroughly enjoy.

He was still telling what I think were jokes –
it was difficult to make out fully formed words –
as I drove him slowly as possible
to hospital.

The Forgetting

The minute I'm appointed Minister
for Justice, Broadcasting, and Espionage,
I'll send forth a decree
making it criminal, and punishable
by being made sit forever
on a bus that never leaves
Kinnegad, to make any further mention of
Miriam O'Callaghan.
It will be an offence
to download any part of Miriam O'Callaghan
from the internet.
Furthermore, any computers or
smart-phones found to contain pictures
of Miriam O'Callaghan
will be broken up
by care-in-the-community
lunatics with specially made
hammers my Department will
provide them with.
The Armed Response Unit will begin
raiding houses known to contain back issues
of the RTE Guide disfigured
with her image.

It will be a crime even
for you to read this poem,
or, technically, for me to have written it.
If reading this poem in the printed version
be sure and eat the paper it's written on
and that all of it has passed successfully
through your digestive system
before you're arrested.

The Case of George Nkencho

If this boy had been more prudently
dropped into life on, say, a street
with trees that throw out their annual yellow
to make a welcome parade for the sun;
had as childhood neighbours a Circuit Court Judge
whose front door had no letter box,
a Garda Chief Inspector with an opinionated
and over-confident dog;
kicked a ball up and down summer evenings,
dead apart from the occasional well behaved bee,
with the boy next door (but one) who blossomed
into a political correspondent
and now gets to make up truth,
another way would've been found.

But for coming at Gardaí
with a chemical imbalance,
what some people are calling
a machete
and a totally inappropriate
post code,
the only sentence
was that ethically administered,
democratically accountable,
bolt action firing squad.

The eminent and learned
bottoms we employ to sit
on the inquiry into this
need not fret the task ahead of them.
For their report is already written.

To The Boys Who Carried Out
The Ballybrit Mosque Attack

You wish you could waddle
up the Monivea Road like Lord Haw Haw
wearing a scar the length of your jaw
you got fighting communists
but cut yourself shaving once
and didn't like it.

In the absence of a girl who'll let
you between her legs
you'd love to invade Russia or Iran
but can't afford the air fare
so instead smashed some glass.

All you want is a part-time job
in the local concentration camp
but there isn't one around here
yet, so instead you broke a window
and heroically chucked some books out it.

You once thought of reading a book
to find out why you're where you are
instead spend the hiatus between
wanks listening to the voices
in the videos on your phone tell you
whose fault your life is.

You needed to be someone
so wrecked a guy's framed family photographs,
fled sniggering up the hill,
still no one.

A Hypochondriac Discusses World Affairs

Why couldn't the burning cathedral
have chosen a better night to go on fire,
than while I'm trying
to cut down on my smoking,
because of the asthma
no doctor can find,
but I know I have?

What will the tick-tock death
of the European Union mean for my hobby
of spending my Januaries vomiting
my way around the Canary Islands
and having the Spanish pay for a doctor
to nod ruefully at me?

What impact, if any, will nuclear war with China
have on my ability to access
alternative remedies from the east
for the crick in the neck
I keep waking up with?

What will the mosque burnt down yesterday –
with a few brown people
running ridiculously around inside it –
mean for my chances
of tonight ordering in a chicken vindaloo
in the hope of making my stomach ulcer
slightly worse?

What effect will the coming walls
of water and fire
have on my sinuses,
which typically don't respond well to either?

And what will it mean for humanity
if, sick of my whingeing,
one of them finally gets the guts
to pick up the cushion
and quietly smother me,
and their little planet ceases to be
because I'm not here to imagine it?

The Bottom of It

I dragged my sinuses doctor to doctor
best part of two decades, and got nowhere.
After that, I tried arthritis but didn't like it.
In later life, I took up hang gliding
in the hope I might break my back
but had to settle for a most unsatisfactory
bout of, what I think was, sciatica.
All this caused my cat such stress
he's taken up smoking five cigars a night,
though I tell him it's doing neither of us
any good. I had my head partially frozen
and then put for five minutes in an oven,
but never quite got to the bottom of it.
Now, for all I know, I could be dead.
But can't be sure. No one's been
around of late to tell me I'm not.
Never one to make a fuss,
I'll just sit here until
someone complains about the smell.

Death Leaves Me Be

I'm plagued instead by the Angel of Not-Yet.
To answer the door
or not to answer the door.
To pull on a ghastly pair of pants
or not to bother.
To both be here
and not be here.
Forever waking up
or thinking about lying down.
The days when I could envisage an alternative career
as an acrobat
or an internationally famous ice-skater
are over.
I hang about the place like evidence
of someone else's terrible mistake.

Clump of Cells

after William Blake

You are, at most, a week or two old.
How big will you grow?
Your potential, vast.
For now you're happy
to skulk there, quietly establishing yourself,
elbowing out of your way
those who lack your secret code.

No one knows you've arrived:
two, four, six, eight
secretly becoming a trillion
while they take you with them on picnics
or give you your first taste of gin and tonic,
though you don't yet officially exist.

Everyone knows your name.
It decorates the headed notepaper
of esteemed charities and titles of reports.
Careers and fortunes are made doing research into you.

But, for now, you are nothing,
a touch of fatigue,
a vague feeling of discomfort
that's probably a pulled muscle.
The second they know you're here
they'll start sweating
and whispering your name
and stop taking you on picnics.
Even if they succeed in killing you
they'll spend forever looking for signs of you.

AstraZeneca

after Brian Patten

Now all the old gods have died
or are on life support in
the prison infirmary psychiatric wing
we have a new name for the absolute:
AstraZeneca. Even those who get
emotional at dinner parties
about the state of the planet
know there's no talking back
to AstraZeneca, the one who now decides
who gets to go outside
and who must remain in the cupboard.

Old women, whose husbands
haven't come back out of
the bedside locker since this time last year,
get down on their bony knees
and ask AstraZeneca to please
keep them in there for good.

The Minister for Exams clasps
her sad hands together and pleads
that AstraZeneca intercede
before she's pushed
through the streets by students
in a shopping trolley
wearing a dunce's hat.

Diplomats, Popes, and
Patriarchs of Constantinople
issue joint communiqués begging
AstraZeneca to save us
from the Russians.

Like most gods, AstraZeneca
has a customer help-line
it never answers.

But we dial it in any case,
our nerve endings electric
at the thought of what
we're at the mercy of.

As the next war starts
every side claims this
new deity belongs to them,
and the streets ring
with the sound of AstraZeneca laughing.

The Unnecessary People

When this world,
and the money with which
you bought it, have been abolished
and all the broken things fixed
and people like me in total control,
you'll be allowed come and go
from your gated community of the unnecessary
so you can see how great the world is without you.

We'll even employ a retired supermodel
to bring you your tea
and, when the time comes, change your nappy.

And buy you a board game
which lets you pretend
to again buy the world
with money that was once real
and absolutely does smell.

And give you a calculator so you can work out what
the corporate tax rate was in places
that no longer go by that name.

And leave on your bedside locker
a note pad in which you can draw pictures
of the spaceship
on which you'll make your final escape.

What The Minister for Housing Proposes: Thinking Outside The Council House

Easy for the Opposition
to hang around overheated TV studios,
spouting impossible promises
which at this stage sound
like a recorded message from Santa Claus.
But out there, in what I like to call
the world, a constituent of mine
and his wheelchair recently spent
the coldest night of the year
in a discontinued telephone box
and, worse than that, there are people
who have nothing better to do
than use this situation as an excuse
to be atrocious to Government Ministers
on Twitter.

If we as a country,
who, relatively speaking, lived mainly
in tumbled-in cottages
and could barely afford trousers
until around about last Friday,
are to get past this glitch
we need to start thinking
outside the traditional council house –
which, like communism,
selling encyclopaedias door to door,
and National Health glasses,
isn't coming back.

First thing tomorrow morning
immediately after my Eggs Benedict
I will introduce tax breaks incentivising
those that have them to rent out every available
wardrobe and wheelie bin
to those who through some bad life
decision have found themselves caught
between tiny thousand quid a month
flats.

Given the lack of such facilities
in your average wheelie bin or wardrobe,
every qualifying adult will be issued with a potty
which may be emptied anywhere except
over the Minister for Housing's head.

And under subsection seven
of my Housing Emergency Provisions act
infants inconsiderate enough to have been born
without fixed abode will be confined
to newly tax deductible sideboard drawers
so they won't grow up
to take more space
than the world has for them.

Backlash by Name

after Nina Simone

The moment you grow too sure
he sends the world into reverse;
one by one, begins taking back
your Christmas presents and keeps
taking until you have less
than you had December the first
the year you were born.

He stuffs you into the boot of a car
and drives you
backward many miles until you're further
from your destination than you were
the day you started out.

He gives you back
all your illnesses at once
but lets you keep the side-effects
of the poison that was going to fix you.

He rents a skip for outside
what was once your house;
lets local children put you
and your opinion
of yourself in it.

He makes your mother
drag herself up out of her grave
and bang the table
as she tells the committee, no
she never heard of you.

To The Man Who Defines Ireland

When telling us, as a nation, to cop on to ourselves
you spit the words Provo
or *workers' paradise* like a lady
trying to rid her mouth of sour milk.

But your voice is church bells and sunshine
pouring down on Kingstown Harbour, circa 1913
when you put your tongue across the syllables
Her Majesty, Queen Elizabeth.

The greatest thing to come out of Crumlin
since the curried chips
that made a young Phil Lynott
question his lifestyle choices.

You are politically and philosophically serious
as a second division footballer's fashion sense,
circa 1977; or a stockbroker last seen exiting
a high-end house of great repute
wearing a thirteen gallon hat;
or a guy in a white linen jacket
who'll end up wandering O'Connell Street
shouting against Home Rule.

And without you, we'd not be ourselves.
For you are our national anticonvulsant
without which we'd be in danger
of actually doing something.

Our Posh Liberal Friends

for Susan

Whenever I show them the Future,
they refuse it;
say: this future has bad hair,
waves its arms around too much,
is too Jewish,
or not Jewish enough,
too not-a-woman,
or the wrong sort of woman.

This Future has a face that one day
might raise the corporate tax rate
by zero point five percent,
and is a little too insistent
that poor people be allowed live,
give or take, as long as the rest of us.
That sort of thing scares the people we dine with
nights we're not dining with you.

I ask the barman for more finger food,
picture the ocean raging into the restaurant,
and them still sat there muttering at the chicken goujons:
the people we talk to won't vote for
such extreme solutions. No one wants to live in Cuba,
one of them says, as she's washed out the door.

I pray, when all the futures
they've turned their noses up at
are safely in the mud
and the men in boots and leather come
to escort us all to the Processing Centre
in the back of a truck
that I be shot, cleanly through the skull, at the front gate,
so I don't suffer their groans
about the quality of the gruel,
and how that last beating one of them got
was clearly in breach of the Human Rights Act
and worthy of a curtly worded,
but still civil, letter to The Observer.

The Problem with History as I've Experienced It

It interferes with the right of people like me
to dine as we see fit.

Whenever I visit England
1649, the sound of it taking just one swing
of an inarticulate axe
to abolish monarchy
puts me off my coffee.
After that, with every mug
I see King Charles'
dripping head being tossed
like a football to a crowd who, I'm sorry,
are all in desperate need of a dentist.

When I land in France at its moment of terror
though I'm up for Liberté, Égalité, Fraternité
in theory
the fact the revolutionaries don't stop
to wipe the blade between chops
makes my l'escargot difficult to digest.

And I've never found a version
of the Haitian slave revolt
during which several exquisite
tankards of rum – of the kind
I aspire to drink –
weren't unnecessarily spilt.

During the burning of Atlanta, wherever I situate
my alfresco table, it's always overthrown
and my black-eyed peas roll
tragically into the oven-like street.
This, Mr Lincoln, I will not forgive.

Similarly, the day of Mr King's march
on Washington, I found the ice cream parlours
impossibly overcrowded.
To such an extent, on the national holiday
that bears his name
I scream for the knickerbocker glories
to which I, as a citizen, am entitled.

And now History's come to visit us here in Portland,
it appalls to find Black Lives Matter –
which I thought I supported – breathing
a little too definitely in our direction,
when my husband just wants
to stroke his humanist beard in peace
while I consider:
which soup?

How to Get Rid of Christopher Columbus

Don't get photographed presenting your
two thousand names to the Mayor,
looking as if you're graduating
with a qualification you'll never use.
Don't ask the Church of Ireland or National Council
for the Advancement of Concerned People
to intervene.

Do it yourself.
But not explosives, no.
There's always a mostly innocent
retired car park attendant with a limp
(or some such) passing at the exact moment.
He retired five years ago
but because of the limp
was still on his way home.
And now he's in small pieces
or, even worse,
one piece;
and you're the reason
he has that stutter
when the journalist talks to him
on the every o'clock news.

Nothing like a spot of terrorism
gone amiss
to make all that racism, pillage, and slicing
off most of a native's thigh
just to test your blades
or a child's hand
because their parents wouldn't cooperate
with what was
an honest attempt to improve them
seem civilised in comparison.

Arm yourself with
no mere plinkety chisel
but mallet, kango hammer,
a couple of the like-minded,
and high vis jackets marked
'City Council' or 'Irish Water'
and present the slow citizenry
with the fact
of his stone tribute
in the sea.

Note From The Organisers

Feel free to turn up (or not)
wearing a full suit of armour,
or a hat with a big feather in it
and transparent trousers;
or to come dressed as a future
Bishop of Cork and Ross,
or as the prophet Isaiah's
discredited older brother.

But this march is no wild ground
on which entrist dandelions
or buttercups will be allowed grow.
The Committee permits
no placards or literature
of a factional variety.
Most egregious those
with crazy words on them,
like "people before profit".

So as not to put off
those not necessarily
in favour of people
(nor at all against profit)
our gathering will resemble
less a revolution
than a church group
on its way somewhere
to pray for a cure
for rheumatism,
or even better,
no cure;

so we can stand here
in increasing discomfort,
become such fixtures
even well behaved
dogs from Dun Laoghaire
start anointing
our legs as public conveniences.

Homage to Henry Kissinger

When Henry Kissinger again fails to die:
    Another tree in the Central Highlands loses all its leaves
    A girl sits on a visiting diplomat's lap
    Someone organises a Nelson Rockefeller look-alike party
    which Henry Kissinger attends
    An election result somewhere is declared null and void for its own good
    An interrogating officer switches on the electricity
    A government spokesman interrupts his denial to wish Dr Kissinger well
    Another tin of Heinz baked beans is sold in China
    and the CEO personally thanks Henry Kissinger
    A ginger cat named Agent Orange leaps down off the garden wall
    A baby slides from the womb with a surprise third arm

When Henry Kissinger again fails to die:
    A ginger cat named Agent Orange leaps back onto its garden wall
    A government we didn't like is overthrown in a military coup,
    welcomed by the European Union
    A hut is set on fire for the greater good,
    the European Union calls for an inquiry
    Someone dies of politically necessary starvation
    but that someone is never Henry Kissinger
    A bomb is dropped on someone whose name you'll never have to pronounce
    because it's not Henry Kissinger

    For its birthday, a baby gets Spina bifida
    A Bengali family have all their arms sawn off.
    Fifty bodies topple into the sea off Indonesia
    but none of them are Henry Kissinger
Each time Henry Kissinger again fails to die.

What You're Saying

I find interesting as a town
in which everyone is Bob Dole;
their spouses, relatives, dogs, and cats also
Bob Dole. Anyone not Bob Dole
refused admittance,
or if they manage to sneak in
immediately deported
for not being Bob Dole
in a place where only
Bob Dole is permitted.

Thought provoking
as a weeklong convention
on the history of the brown paper bag
in a city without cocktails, massage parlours,
or even as much as a cup of tea.
But lots of brown paper bags
and people who know things
about brown paper bags.

Thrilling, even, as driving
down a back road with nothing on it
to Borris-in-Ossory
at thirty miles an hour
every day for a hundred years while listening
to Gina, Dale Haze, and The Champions'
Greatest Hits on a loop,
and not being offered the possible release
of being allowed die at the wheel.

2152

after Sophie Hannah

It's 2152 and Cumbria's declared independence
after a campaign during which they blew
bits of Princess Eugenie all over
Lake Windermere. There's a free market
in carcasses throttled by the latest mutant.
On Newsnight Kirsty Wark mutters from her crypt:
we may have run out of ambulances,
but at least we dodged the bullet that was Corbyn.

London's dead have mostly been snapped up by a Russian oligarch
with a place overlooking Hyde Park
and a lifelong interest in taxidermy. Tonight he's away to a party
where he hopes to be introduced to the late Eddie Izzard
who, despite being dead, still sits on Labour's National Executive.

Mock The Week is seven skeletons rattling
in unison at something one of them belched
about Diane Abbott. The country's now being led
by one of Andrew Neil's more senior pubic lice. On the BBC
Suzanne Moore's hair and the new strain of bacteria
they found on Tony Parsons agree:
at least it's not Corbyn.

Brits from the six disease ridden bits
into which the Kingdom's now splintered
have been barred from entering Bulgaria, Guatemala, Yemen...
But news of this is drowned by Ian Hislop's skull chuckling
at something Andrew, Duke of York,
now reincarnated as a fungus, just said about Corbyn.

Jess Phillips hasn't blown her trombone in
a hundred and thirty two years. And Starmer's
deported so many Jews from the Labour Party*
he's received a congratulatory telegram from IG Farben.
He shared it just now on Twitter as proof
he's not Corbyn.

---

* Since he became leader of the British Labour Party two years ago, Keir Starmer has
expelled more Jewish people from the party than all other previous Labour leaders com-
bined, many of them on charges of "anti-Semitism"

The Candidate Explains

after Charlotte Nichols MP

I didn't know the meaning
of "incursion" or "dealt with"
the negative connotation until this morning.
Didn't realise the possible definitions
of "parasite", "rubbish dump", "bad human material".
Didn't know until this morning the connotations
of "dismantle", "pikey", "assimilate".
The negative meanings of "scum",
"child thief", "branding iron".
Didn't know "dirty", "asocial", "expel".
The connotations of "a people involved
in the manufacture of human freaks."
Didn't know the meaning until now
of "Rahoonery", "pollutant", "Pharajimos".
The problematic side of those over the age of five
being taken away and civilised.
Didn't know the meaning of "The Devouring",
"The Cutting Up", or "behind concrete walls".
The negative connotation of "whoever kills one,
shall be guilty of nothing."
Didn't know the meaning of "deport"
until I saw it done this morning,
clean as a Police Superintendent's signature
or a Councillor's campaign for re-election.

And Now For The Good News

The ocean is five percent less on fire
than it would be if they'd elected the other guy.
No new viruses have leapt from the Amazon
so far today. Or if they have
we don't yet know their names.
And it's already lunchtime.
So we must live in hope.

The G7 summit has given the nod
to lobbing no more missiles
than absolutely necessary
at Russian and Chinese ships
in the Sea of Azov and Taiwan Strait.

Closer to home, the latest
by-election has been won
by a nice lady everyone agrees
is no threat to anything.

And the doctor assures me
I'll be safely in the ground
before the two hundred mile an hour
winds tear the roof off the house
as if stripping open a tin of fish.

Administration

I

Please complete the enclosed
form number 204A,
though it's the wrong one
for your purposes; return it to me
no later than tomorrow
when we'll be closed all day
for staff straining.
When you find me not here,
pop it in the letter box
and worry that I never received it.

Please be advised,
given current market conditions,
about which I know nothing,
we generally refuse applications
such as yours in advance. Though
in every other way a nobody;
when it comes to the little things,
like your life,
my decision is final.

II

Born in different days,
I could've sat at a fatter desk than this
counting the Jews
in Czarist Russia, or helping
the Hapsburgs ensure
the train to Bratislava
always ran late.
We are victims of circumstance,
all of us. And I am the circumstance
in which you now find yourself.

My aim in life
that clock striking five;
to get safely out of here
and not know for sure
that my immediate superior
is using the office beneath me –
locked since Friday,
October 21st, 1994 –
to store genetically modified
women imported
on false Lithuanian passports,
which I never saw.

Apologies

To any white South Africans hurt
by the anti-Apartheid movement.
To any tobacco plantation owner's son barred
by Emancipation from dragging his father's
private property for a spot of fish-eyed non-consensual
in a barn that has seen it all,
despite the absolute lack of light in there.
To General Custer for any inconvenience
caused by the tribes who sent him home
by a road he did not know.
To any Frenchmen or women
savages with Russian guns robbed
of their own personal slice of Algeria.
To any Havana casino owners or pimps offended
by the extent of Fidel Castro's facial hair.
To the small part of Ian Paisley Junior that dies
every time someone calls Judea and Samaria
or Londonderry by its proper name.
To any cats hurt by mice
who didn't lie down and just
let themselves be eaten.

The Most Risk-Taking Poet In Ireland

My split infinitives clearly the work of a man
who dries his clothes recklessly,
sometimes not emptying the lint tray
two cycles in a row.

At the height of my experiments with formal verse
I once drove a Ford Focus
at a tantalising twenty nine kilometres per hour
when the legal limit was thirty.

During my decadent prose-poem phase
I tiptoed past a locked apartment door,
behind which, I'm pretty sure,
there was an orgy going on.

Under the influence of Samuel Taylor Coleridge,
I once took one more paracetamol
than I should have.

In a rare outbreak of concrete poetry,
I yesterday regrouted the shower tiles myself.

Trying to mimic Rimbaud vanishing in Abyssinia,
back when I was young and even more foolish
than this, I once accidentally went
to Dorset.

My contribution to metaphor
in the twenty first century
is at least as important
as the cat yawning.

Risk, for me, is going
to a different garden centre
at least once every five years.

Creative Writing – Induction Speech

It's not all hanging around the college bar
pretending to be Ted and Sylvia;
or escaping to Italy with your lover,
like the Barrett Brownings;
or head-butting rivals in the green room
during what you'll later call
your Norman Mailer phase;
or leaving your top hat behind you
in the brothel that week you thought
you were Baudelaire.

Most don't soar
up the Times best seller list
on their way to being given
an award by Prince Edward.
Not everyone can be the next
Ocean Vuong. Or the
Ocean Vuong after that.
And critical acclaim after you're dead
won't buy you the tiniest
bag of Hula Hoops at Tesco's.
You'll likely have to diversify.

When you leave here you'll have the ability
to lie more plausibly to detectives
and make up dossiers
about Liechtenstein's secret
nuclear weapons programme.

Others of you will graduate to be entrepreneurs
who sell bags of badness, imported via Amsterdam
up other people's orifices or stowed away
in their stomachs to emerge gloriously later,
but never use an unnecessary adjective.

At least one of you will likely become a hit woman
who always has the perfect closing line,
and be known to both victims and those
who sent you to their door as The Poet.

And a few will mature into waistcoats who get high
typing pungent updates about drunk women you spy
squatting in shop doorways
with binoculars you bought courtesy of your *Writer's
Bursary For The Partially Sighted.*

My Approach to Literary Networking

after Francois Villon

Most days I'd rather be bundled
into the courthouse between
two hairy policemen,
with a highly debatable anorak
dragged over my face, and
blamed for killing Kirov –
the crowd lobbing big thick
spits and battering the van
as I'm carted off –

or be stopped at the Canadian border
travelling on a makey up Polish passport,
the remnants of a Dutch industrialist
and what I think was his second wife settled
unhappily in my glove compartment;

or attend my mother-in-law's funeral
having been fitted with a wooden nose
because (everybody knows)
the other one fell off due to
third stage syphilis;

than ghost about the joint provoking
nods from gabardine coats
of great import and longevity,
grunts of approval
from fully clothed minor male poets.

We Lie

after Holly McNish

My one remaining friend,
now I've plugged out my Mum,
is in my pretend life
because he's willing to not notice
what I metaphorically call
things. Like the fact that I carry about with me,
smiling up out of my man-bag,
a two day dead pike
that looks like it died
of a personality disorder;
had its oily head beaten in by someone
who could take no more
of it blathering on
in a fake south London accent
about how it was finking of voting
Lib Dem, and that it heard
the lyrics on Adele's post-divorce album
are surprisingly upbeat.

My friend is still my friend
'cos unlike all the ex-people
I had to drop concrete blocks on
he's able to let on
my succession of pet dead pikes
don't smell because his nose
has grown so used to
dead pike at this stage
he'd miss it if it wasn't
there to block out
the even smellier
dead things that live
at the bottom of my man-bag,
the leather existence of which
you must be prepared to deny
even when questioned by psychiatrists,
if you want to be my friend.

Essay on Vagueness

after Ocean Vuong

Because the poodle's polka dot collar
lying luminous at the bottom of the stairs
was an exclamation mark
discarded from a poem.
Because all your relatives
kept turning up—& the kettle
exploded from our over use.
So I gathered mouthfuls
of soil, dark as an Iraq veteran's toenails,
and spat it out
like crazy black toothpaste into
a bicycle helmet
little enough to keep safe
my idea of myself.
Because at the funfair I aimed
for the target and failed
to win you the teddy bear
you would have named Jonah—
instead tore off for you
a leg of roast chicken
despite knowing
you're vegan and only eat,
from the clay plate you knitted yourself,
the end result of photosynthesised light.
I will take you nowhere
but go everywhere myself
dressed like this.
Because I, too,
need an interpreter
to make sense of me
and pour my Chai tea. So I held my nose
with what I believed were
your fingers and leapt
into the seaweed bath, sawed open
the tin of tuna you brought me

and set all the fish free.
My mouth was a wound
that had healed over
and I could open it no more,
until I ran around the place
screaming in every
pair of shorts I've ever worn
& it was done.
& I was poetry.

The Shipping Forecast

Back when the three giant liners,
Britannia, Eurasia, and Sweet Land of Liberty
weren't all simultaneously
taking on tonnes of water,
you didn't have to think
about what makes them float.

After loading your gut at the buffet
with more prawns and chocolate cheesecake
than it could be trusted to process –
each prawn pausing to give you
a filthy look before it slid
down your in-pipe –
you'd relax on the deck
of whichever of these
great ships you had a ticket for,
sip a glass of alleged
sophistication, as a talking
corduroy jacket
at the table next to you
waxes loud and large
about cheap insurance
policies and the invincibility
of ships such as this.

Now you've speed-read the technical manuals
and know
if certain particulars aren't fixed
we're all going to die
or, at least, want to;
you look at the corduroy
jackets talking their opinions
and wonder if it's better
to be like them;
to think the answer
might be to elect as captain
some demagogue made of blancmange
or, failing that, Joe Biden;

or if not knowing just makes the shock
of the ocean hugging you
that bit worse?

'Liberals' &'Death'

Two words that strut confident of
their own historical inevitability.
Everyone in time meets them,
though hopefully not both
ringing your door bell
the same day,
unless your name is
Nagasaki or Vietnam;

or you're the first village
no-one's ever heard of
successfully abolished
from thirty thousand feet
by a transgender person
pressing a button;

or you're the first Somali in history
proudly turned into a pile of burning mince
by a drone designed by a woman of colour;

or you're the wrong type of Australian
whose computer told us the names
of the obliterated
and so can only leave prison
in a fair-trade cardboard box.

Island

after Wislawa Szymborska

Where men with shiny scalps
fight for the right to dye
hair they no longer have
any colour they want.

Here, garbage can by magicked
into its opposite by the mere act
of attaching to it the word: Great.

Proud nation that pays
redundant assembly-line operatives
to sell photo-shopped versions of itself
to tourists from its former colonies.

Raised voices in its cathedral city tea rooms.
So shrill a cup gets chipped
in the course of the argument
and a scone is left behind on the plate.

The roses around its cottage gates try to forget.
But, elsewhere, the dead factory remembers.

And the disgraced estate agent tries to secure the door
on what was once British Home Stores
but can't fathom the lock.

Febrile

"I am the Empire in the last of its decline."
Paul Verlaine

I am Britain in the final orgasm of its fall,
that watches the confident Scots and Irish
pack their bright new suitcases
and stride palely towards the exit,
like soon-to-be ex-wives
that would be the death of me,
if I weren't already dead.

The chalk cliffs of Dover
have been sold to a Chinese consortium
and the front pages applaud the deal
as a great victory.

Andrew Loyd Webber has been forced
at pistol point to write additional verses
for Rule Britannia.

I flip the pages of the atlas and imagine
invading places here, there
with the help of aircraft carriers
I no longer have but can still,
just about, picture.

On Gran Canaria withered Englishmen celebrate
their independence and look forward
to having to dress their own bed sores
in second hand bandages they'll get free
with every glass of Weatherspoon's
English sparking wine.

Aurum

chemical element with symbol Au
(from Latin: aurum) and atomic number 79

Days petroleum is selling for not even the cost
of taking it out of the ground
and putting it in a Toyota Corolla;
the world takes refuge in you.

Hope of you persuades people
to invest in a prototype hat with a propeller
that just might be the twenty first century way
of transporting oneself to the office.

You can get a woman a third kidney
to keep on ice, just in case;
or purchase for a family
most of central Kiev and new faces
even worse than what
they were born with, and because of you
no one will tell them they're ugly.

You can buy a ticket that makes it okay
to be what would otherwise be
the wrong colour, or one foot three
tall with no teeth,
as long as the ticketholder
makes up for such deficiencies
with their fabulous wit
on Graham Norton.

You can fetch a woman a new bronze
husband named Brad,
trained to just stand there smiling
in his swimming trunks,
until the elastic eventually snaps.

You endow universities on condition
they pretend the children of the giver
are intelligent; great physicists who just happened
to end up editing fashion magazines
given them by Dad.

Enough of you can buy
any part of woman or child;
get for everyone
their own personal Venezuela.
And should some jumped-up gurrier
nick it off them,
give them the means to snatch it
rightfully back.

Shiniest metal ever ripped
from riverbed or mine.
You decorate the second wives of the rich
with nooses made of twenty four carat you;
or lurk uselessly in vaults.
And when everyone in town is bought
you go in search of other worlds to purchase.

All The Angel of History Sees Now

"His face is turned toward the past."
Walter Benjamin

The leaping orange
of make-do cremations in New Delhi car parks,
the bones being taken away to be crushed;
the Cold Blob loitering in the far north,
planning who knows what for the weather;
the National Park only slightly
less on fire than yesterday;
bargain slave children to be had
in the market squares of
newly liberated Libya.

His eyes never settle on what
the things he witnesses will overthrow,
what they will force to be born

bawling its purple jowled displeasure
at being expelled from the quiet life
into a future it cannot know
but must nevertheless make.

Past

Past clicks ajar the box
you thought you'd locked it in
and starts walking in your direction.
Under its right arm, it carries a kitten
you'd thought long dead
which is delighted to see you
and licks your hand
in the hope of butter or salt.
Past fishes your friend out of whichever
European river he went into
and deletes the message
you got from his cousin asking
if you've seen him.
His hair, still the same
Judas Iscariot red.
Yours, its increasingly inferior
imitation of its ex-self.
You talk hours
about coming revolution
which, like the kitten,
you remember burying
but which now magically offers you
an opening comradely hand.
Past takes its spade
and digs up your old defeats,
offers to turn them into victories
if you're prepared to gamble
on losing again
and pain which even now haunts,
like the tooth you tried
but failed to extract yourself.

Acknowledgements

Acknowledgements are due to the following magazines, websites, & anthologies in which versions of these poems first appeared:

The Moth; *Skylight 47*; *The Poets' Republic*; *The New European* (UK); *Japanese Journal of Irish Studies*; *Orbis* (UK); *Village Magazine*; *The Cormorant*; *The Waxed Lemon*; *Poetry & All That Jazz* (UK); *Live Encounters*; *The Honest Ulsterman*; *Abridged*; *Ink, Sweat & Tears* (UK); *Prole*; *Boyne Berries*; *Crannóg*; *ROPES*; *Vox Galvia – The Galway Advertiser*; *Spilling Cocoa Over Martin Amis*; *Rochford Street Review* (Australia); *Communion* (Australia); *The Blue Nib*; Broadsheet.ie; Clare Daly MEP's Facebook page; *The Platform* (UK); *Culture Matters* (UK); *Cassandra Voices*; *The Satirist* (USA); *The Ogham Stone*; *The Pickled Body*; *The Stony Thursday Book*; *The Canadian Journal of Irish Studies*; *Labour Against The Witch Hunt*; *The Poetry Village*; *The Frogmore Papers* (UK); *Owl of Minerva*; *Days of Clear Light: A Festschrift for Jessie Lendennie and in Celebration of Salmon Poetry at 40* (Eds Nessa O'Mahony & Alan Hayes, published by Salmon Poetry); *Black Lives Matter: Poems For A New World* (Civic Leicester, UK), & *We're All in it Together: Poems for a DisUnited Kingdom* (Grist Books, UK).

'What The Minister for Housing Proposes: Thinking Outside The Council House' was commissioned for the BBC Radio 4 documentary *My Modest Proposal*. 'The Ten Great Wisdoms' was broadcast on YouTube by Galway County Library Service for Poetry Day Ireland 2021. '2152' & 'The Most Risk-Taking Poet In Ireland' were broadcast on the online political show Not PMQs.

KEVIN HIGGINS is co-organiser of Over The Edge literary events in Galway. He has published five previous full collections of poems: *The Boy With No Face* (2005), *Time Gentlemen, Please* (2008), *Frightening New Furniture* (2010), *The Ghost In The Lobby* (2014), and *Sex and Death at Merlin Park Hospital* (2019). His poems also feature in *Identity Parade: New British and Irish Poets* (Bloodaxe, 2010) and in *The Hundred Years' War: modern war poems* (Ed Neil Astley, Bloodaxe May 2014). Kevin was satirist-in-residence with the alternative literature website *The Bogman's Cannon* 2015-16. *2016 – The Selected Satires of Kevin Higgins* was published by NuaScéalta in 2016. *The Minister For Poetry Has Decreed* was published by Culture Matters (UK) also in 2016. *Song of Songs 2:0: New & Selected Poems* was published by Salmon in Spring 2017. Kevin is a highly experienced workshop facilitator and several of his students have gone on to achieve publication success. He has facilitated poetry workshops at Galway Arts Centre and taught Creative Writing at Galway Technical Institute for the past fifteen years. Kevin is the Creative Writing Director for the NUI Galway International Summer School and also teaches on the NUIG BA Creative Writing Connect programme. His poems have been praised by, among others, Tony Blair's biographer John Rentoul, *Observer* columnist Nick Cohen, writer and activist Eamonn McCann, historian Ruth Dudley Edwards, and *Sunday Independent* columnist Gene Kerrigan; and have been quoted in *The Daily Telegraph, The Independent, The Times* (London), *Hot Press* magazine, *The Daily Mirror* and on *The Vincent Browne Show*, and read aloud by Ken Loach at a political meeting in London. He has published topical political poems in publications as various as *The New European, The Morning Star, Dissent Magazine* (USA), *Village Magazine* (Ireland), & *Harry's Place. The Stinging Fly* magazine has described Kevin as "likely the most widely read living poet in Ireland". One of Kevin's poems features in *A Galway Epiphany*, the final instalment of Ken Bruen's Jack Taylor series of novels which is just published. His work has been broadcast on RTE Radio, Lyric FM, and BBC Radio 4. His book *The Colour Yellow & The Number 19: Negative Thoughts That Helped One Man Mostly Retain His Sanity During 2020* was published in late 2020 by Nuascealta. His extended essay 'Thrills & Difficulties: Being A Marxist Poet In 21st Century Ireland' was published in pamphlet form by Beir Bua Press in 2021. *Ecstatic* is Kevin's sixth full poetry collection.

salmonpoetry

Cliffs of Moher, County Clare, Ireland

"Publishing the finest Irish and international literature."
Michael D. Higgins, President of Ireland